YES

— IS THE —

ANSWER

How Positivity, Passion, and
Pineapples Will Transform
Your Leadership and Your Life

CHRISTINE TRIPPI

The Wise Pineapple

Published by The Wise Pineapple LLC

Cover design by Mike Trippi

Print ISBN: 978-1-7332440-1-5

Paperback ISBN: 978-1-7332440-2-2

eBook ISBN: 978-1-7332440-0-8

For information about this title or to order other books and/or electronic media, contact the publisher:

The Wise Pineapple LLC

www.thewisepineapple.com

Praise for Christine Trippi and
Yes Is the Answer

"Passion changes everything! Christine Trippi's passion and simple approach to responding positively will inspire you to become a first-in-class hotelier. *Yes Is the Answer* is a must read for any leader, especially anyone in the business of hospitality."

—**Anthony Melchiorri,** president of Argeo Hospitality, host and executive producer of Hotel Impossible and Five Star Secrets

---

"If you are in any kind of hospitality business, this book is for you. Become the place everyone can't wait to come back to. Have employees that every competitor wants to recruit. Get recognized for being 'The Best in Town!' Buy this book NOW—and jumpstart building your brand into one of the World's Best!"

—**"Famous Dave" Anderson**, America's Rib King and BBQ Hall of Fame

"Everyone in the hospitality industry—and any industry, for that matter—should invest a few hours and read *Yes Is the Answer.* Christine Trippi exemplifies a person who always leads from her heart and seeks to create wonderful experiences for guests and everyone she encounters. It's this positive mindset that lays the foundation for success and happiness in business and life … and now you can experience *Yes Is the Answer*—the simple approach that can get you there."

—**Danny Bader**, bestselling author and inspirational speaker, *I Met Jesus for a Miller Lite, Abraham's Diner*, and *Back from Heaven's Front Porch*

"*Yes Is the Answer* is not just an easy-to-read-and-apply book, it is an inspiration; it is a how-to manual; it is a manifesto of brilliance; and it is full of results-getting insights, experiences, research, and pro tips to help take you, your team, and your business to the next level! If you are at all interested and serious about becoming the best of the best, this is a MUST READ!"

—**Brandon W. Johnson**, aka Positive Energy Guy, award-winning author/speaker/trainer, named the #1 Global Guru for the hospitality industry in 2017 & 2018

"Say YES to this book and capture the strategies for creating a lasting legacy of exceptional service in your organization. You will laugh, cry, and be part of changing the world one YES at a time!"

—**Jon Vroman**, founder of FrontRowFoundation.org and FrontRowDads.com and author of *The Front Row*

"I have worked with Christine and watched her work her magic of *Yes Is the Answer* firsthand. In this book, you will learn practical ways to apply this positive philosophy to literally any industry, even in your personal relationships. As both an HR professional and as an Executive Search professional, I have worked side by side with her, hired her, and represented her. I am delighted to see her put her actions into a book to share! Read it; it will change the way you view many obstacles both at work and in your own life!"

—**Peggy Olson**, managing partner at Carver-Olsen Hospitality Search

"Yes Is the Answer is a wonderful book to help empower my team! Although this book is based in a hotel, we definitely are going to implement these 4 steps in my medical practice! If a patient comes into our office not feeling well, we now have some skills to help them feel better even before they see our healthcare provider. From simply making an appointment for an irate patient to dealing with an anxious patient when the doctor is running late from an emergency, these skills can apply to almost anything! We are now going to brainstorm with my team about the common conflicts and foresee any other possible conflicts to develop strategies and solutions. Thank you, Christine Trippi, for giving me some key skills in improving the healthcare of my patients through better 'bedside manner.' I highly recommend this book to anyone dealing with customers in any industry, which means patients for me!"

—**Richard A. Mojares**, MD, FAAP, FACP and medical director, Family First Urgent Care

"There are many books that teach us how to say 'no' as a time management strategy. What they don't teach is how to avoid the uncomfortable feelings associated with another's potential rejection from that answer. Ms. Trippi's suggestions are powerful and invaluable ways to build relationships, win loyalty, and make emotional connections that make the difference!"

—**Len Ghilani**, President Ghilani Group

Sweet Dedication:

To my Mom and Pops, June and Carl Chase, the ones who started it all with their never-ending love and support. Thank you for always being there to remind me—whenever I thought a challenge was too great—that once upon a time, I thought I couldn't steak-walk. (You'll understand that if you ever worked at Ponderosa.)

To my babies, Spencer and Samantha Trippi, nobody has taught me more about life than both of you. If I could, I would raise you both all over again. I'll love you forever! And to my "Honey Bunny," Mike Trippi, you have painted my life with bright, bold, and happy colors, and I'm so thankful I walked into the Flipside and purchased "Brown-Eyed Girl". I love you!

Special thanks to my sisters and niece, Ginny Kissamis, Jessica Avila, and Addie Bowers, for believing in me and helping me understand why I can't put commas anywhere I want. (I still don't get it!)

Finally, I dedicate this book to Christopher Pasquini for showing us all how to live at 110%. I love you! R.I.P.

SECTION ONE:
INTRODUCTION

What kind of fruit are you?

Did you know the pineapple is the symbol of hospitality?

I wrote this book to inspire you to *Be a Wise Pineapple*—Stand Tall (*Be Confident*), Wear a Crown (*Be Empowered*), and Be Sweet (*Lead from the Heart*).

The pineapple is a symbol of hospitality.

Be a Pineapple:

STAND TALL
(Be Confident)

WEAR A CROWN
(Be Empowered)

BE SWEET
(Lead from the Heart)

CHANGING THE WORLD, ONE YES AT A TIME

My Why

I want to change the world through *Sweet Hospitality*!

I began working in the hotel industry at the young age of 17. The first time I received a letter from one of my guests thanking me for making a genuine difference, I was hooked. I became captivated by making people happy.

When I took that letter home and showed it to my parents, they were very proud. That's when I sat across the kitchen table from the greatest man I've ever known—my dad—and he told me the story about making a difference, one starfish at a time.

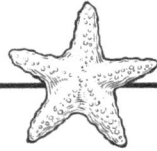

THE STARFISH STORY

An old man was walking on the beach one morning after a storm. In the distance, he could see someone moving like a dancer. As he came closer, he saw that it was a young woman picking up starfish and gently throwing them back into the ocean.

"Young lady, why are you throwing starfish into the ocean?"

"The sun is up and the tide is going out, and if I do not throw them in, they will die," she said.

"But young lady, do you not realize that there are many miles of beach and thousands of starfish? You cannot possibly make a difference."

The young woman listened politely, then bent down, picked up another starfish, and threw it into the sea.

"I made a difference for that one."

Adapted from the original by Loren Eiseley

My dad's message spoke to my heart and from that day forward, I had my purpose. Whether it was a small act of kindness, like a compliment, or something larger like setting up a special surprise for a guest, I planned to change the world by living with positive intentions and making every interaction count.

It's now been more than 30 years since I began my career. (*Please, don't do the math!*) I started this journey as a laundry attendant/van driver at a Hampton Inn in Illinois, and I've held positions from line-level associate to senior management in select service, full service, and resort hotels. I've traveled across this beautiful country operationally supporting, motivating, and facilitating training for hotel teams and leaders. Of all my accomplishments, including being named the General Manager of the Year for Courtyard by Marriott Hotels, and even meeting the legend himself, Mr. Bill Marriott, *nothing* has been more rewarding than knowing I've played a role in shaping our future leaders. It has been my ultimate pleasure to start them on their personal journeys and let them know that they, too, hold the power to change the world.

Each time I shared the Starfish Story, I observed how it touched the person or class I was speaking to. However, once I explained how they could get there through the **Yes *Is the Answer*** philosophy and shared real-life stories, that's when the dots would connect for them, and I could feel their energy. I could see *they* were hooked, too!

At least once a week, I will have a past associate, colleague, or friend reach out to me in some form or fashion and say, "Christine, I have an amazing *Yes* story to tell you!" It's humbling and it's what I'm most proud of. To be inspired is great, but to inspire is AWESOME!

As a hospitality professional, if I could give two gifts to all customer service providers, it would be the awareness that they have the power to change the world and the ability to respond positively to every interaction. That enables them to always Stand Tall (*Be Confident*), Wear a Crown (*Be Empowered*), and Be Sweet (*Lead from the Heart*). This is what I call being a *Wise Pineapple*! And that is how you achieve *Sweet Hospitality, Sweet Cultures, and Sweet Results.*

When Yes Changes Someone's World

I probably have thousands of *Yes* stories from the past 30 years, but one in particular is very special to me.

It was a sunny day at KeyLime Cove Water Resort in Gurnee, Illinois, and my team started gathering early for our morning meeting, as our guests didn't usually stir until about 9 a.m. Just as we were huddling up, I saw a mom and her two boys approaching Mangrove Jack's, our sundries and snack shop. Mangrove's didn't open until 8 a.m., however, so I asked my team to hold a moment so I could greet this family. Since I lead with my heart and live by the *Yes Is the Answer* philosophy, I didn't respond by apologizing, "I'm sorry, Mangrove's doesn't open until 8 a.m." I made friends first and greeted her warmly. I asked if she was here celebrating.

She replied, "As a matter of fact, we are! My boys' birthdays are today. They're twins!"

I thought, "Oh, boy! This is the stuff I live for!" I asked if it would be okay if my team and I had some fun celebrating with the boys, and she was all in. Her smile could have lit up the moon!

We brought the boys into the middle of our huddle, and the whole team did our special birthday cheer ... twice! The boys loved it, and I knew we had just created a special moment for this family. After our fun, we got the boys extra tokens for the arcade and birthday stickers to wear throughout the day, so they would be recognized and celebrated all day long. I helped their mom with the item she needed at Mangrove's, and I asked if it would be okay if I set up a special surprise in their room later. She was very grateful, and the happy family went on their way.

When I got back to our huddle, the whole team was beaming. You see, *Yes* moments work both ways—they create happiness for the recipients *and* the moment-makers! This encounter totally pumped up my team's morning motivation, and I could see they were ready for more. So, we each made a commitment to find at least one other guest during our shift to create a *Yes* moment for, and we also decided that we weren't done with our special birthday twins!

After the water park opened, a few of us went to the family's room and set up one of my *splash-tacular* in-room scavenger hunts. At the end of the hunt, the boys received more birthday surprises, tokens, and a certificate for a Kitchen Sink Sundae from D.W. Anderson's Eatery. We were giddy all day thinking about how much they were going to love it. As I wrapped up my day, I heard a knock on my office door. It was our special mom, but without her boys. She asked if I had a quick moment, and of course, I responded, "*Yes!*"

She said, "Christine, I cannot thank you enough for your kindness today. You truly have made this a wonderful day for me and for my boys. You see, we're here trying to make this day special again because their dad died on the boys' birthday last year." My heart sank. As I recall this story, I can still see her curly brown hair, big glasses, and the tears that collected in her eyes—*mine, too.*

Obviously, we all had no idea how much we were impacting this family when we started our day. We thought we were just having fun helping two little five-year-olds feel special on their birthday. That's the thing—you never know how much the simplest act of kindness or positive *Yes* answer can make a difference to someone and change their day and even their world. We talked a little more and gave each other a huge, tight hug, and when she was leaving she said, "It really *is* a sunny day at KeyLime Cove!"

There it is, my friend! This is what this hospitality gig is all about. We don't just serve food, clean rooms, and check people in. Each and every day we are given opportunities to make a difference and change the world one *Yes* at a time.

The Power of Yes—Sweet Results!

The **Yes Is the Answer** philosophy has changed my life in so many ways, but mostly it has enabled me to be positive, proactive, and solution-based rather than negative, reactionary, and victim-based. It's these skills that have helped me achieve award-winning results and build amazing leaders. They can help you too, no matter what your title!

I first began implementing the **Yes Is the Answer** philosophy by training my own teams, and the *Sweet Results* quickly became evident: increased guest service scores, associate satisfaction, and occupancy. My associates were becoming competent and confident leaders, and my guests were happy, loyal, and telling others! My team at the Marriott Chicago Northwest was consistently ranked in the top 10 of all Marriott Hotels for arrival experience, and the hotel won the "Hotel of the Year" award in 2005. At the Residence Inn, we took our guest service ranking from 377th out of 600-plus hotels to 11th for overall satisfaction. We achieved these *Sweet Results* in only six months.[1]

At one Courtyard where I worked, our team was ranked number one on Trip Advisor in all of Lake County, and 48th out of *1000* Courtyard Hotels (*That's the top 5 percent!*) for overall satisfaction. That Courtyard Hotel was 29 years old and had previously been a red-zone property (below the expected threshold for service). However, with essentially the same team who made it red, we made it GREEN by changing the culture and purpose and by employing the *Yes Is the Answer* philosophy. I like to say that it's not about your four walls, it's about *who is in* your four walls that makes the difference.

My Mission

I've presented my philosophy to all levels of organizations from C-suite executives to line-level associates. Every time, the participants were surprised by how simple it is to answer positively. Every. Single. Time. It wasn't long before I realized that, if I was in this industry to change the world, I needed to get *Yes Is the Answer* out *into* the world.

Along the way, leadership-level participants recognized that, while they may have been telling their own associates that *Yes Is the Answer*, they weren't teaching them *how* to say *Yes*. How could they? They didn't know themselves. Unless you know these simple steps, saying *Yes* can be a challenging game.

I've been told time and time again from countless participants that the information they took away from one of my trainings was some of the best they'd ever received and that it meant so much to them.

After consistently receiving overwhelmingly positive feedback, it was clear that I needed to take it to the next level by getting this information into YOUR hands!

In the whirlwind that is the hospitality world, as well as our vast and varied responsibilities, my goal in creating this book is to produce a bite-sized tool focused on the message that *Yes Is the Answer*, making it easy for you to share with your own teams, colleagues, and friends. I am a strong believer in what Simon Sinek said: *"Simple ideas are easier to understand. Ideas that are easier to understand are repeated. Ideas that are repeated change the world."* And that's the goal, right?

When you adopt the *Yes Is the Answer* philosophy, it can help you increase customer satisfaction, generate more sales, be an empowered and confident leader, and add positivity in your organization as well as to your daily life. Here's the best part: You'll get to CHANGE THE WORLD, one *Yes* at a time. And if *you're buyin' what I'm sellin'*, you're gonna LOVE the information I'm about to share with you.

One more thing—being known as the Director

of Fun, I always try to inject levity and humor into all of my live trainings, and I knew that if I was going to share this information with you, I had to deliver it with that same level of energy and passion. So, I'll be throwing in some of my *"Trip-tacular Vernacular." (Just for fun, there's even a glossary in the back of the book.)* And, in each chapter, I've included a *Sweet Spot* for you to reflect and practice your **Yes Is the Answer** skills. Each time you find a way to say *Yes*, color in your pineapple and let it shine! For those of you reading on an eBook, you can download a complimentary companion workbook on my website at www.the-wisepineapple.com, along with other *free-sources!* Remember to share your #YesIstheAnswer moments on social. Tag me and use the hashtag when you use your Pineapple Power!

This book is intended to be interactive and exude the enthusiasm of one of my live work-shops, and I hope you feel my spirit on every page!

Whoop, Whoop! Let's get started!

---

1. Believe it or not, I almost didn't accept the position at the Residence Inn because it meant I would also be leading housekeeping. Front of the house was my passion, and I

didn't think housekeeping was very sexy! After being in the job for a bit, I discovered that running housekeeping was my absolute favorite part of the job. Learning how I could impact others, including guests and associates, through our guest rooms and the back of the house (also known as the heart of the house) was one of the best experiences of my career. This taught me two things: 1) You don't have to *find* your passion to be happy. Simply *bring* your passion to whatever you are doing. And 2) If it scares the hell out of you, take the job and move out of your comfort zone—the lessons are priceless!

> Your mind is a
> powerful thing.
> When you fill it with
> positive thoughts,
> your life will start to
> change.

JOHN ASSARAF

2

THE LEGEND

Before we begin this journey together, let me tell you about how it all got started. As a young professional leader in the early 1990s, I found myself driven toward excellence and thirsty for advice and direction. While I was working for the Crowne Plaza Hotel in Lisle, Illinois, as the front office manager, I read an article in the newspaper about a hospitality professional who had just received a promotion.

He took his family out to dinner to celebrate this very happy occasion. He told them they could order anything they wanted; this was a special event! After their meal, it was time for the best part— DESSERT! When the server asked his daughter what she would like, she asked for a pineapple milkshake. The waitress responded, "Oh no, I'm sorry, we don't have milkshakes on the menu." The little girl was disappointed, of course, but so was her father. Sure, he was let down because he wanted his family to have whatever they wanted for this celebration, but as someone in the customer service industry that prided himself on providing great service, he was most disappointed in the lack of creativity and empowerment exhibited by this young lady. Pineapple milkshakes may not have been on the menu, but it only takes milk, ice cream, and pineapples to make one. Most restaurants have these basic ingredients on hand, so how hard would it have been to make a pineapple milkshake? This gentleman understood that in our industry, it's important to **Be Creative**, resourceful, and empowered in order to meet the needs and wants of our customers.

This experience impacted him so much that he went back to his hotel and held a big team rally where he told everyone about his encounter with the waitress. He declared from that day forward that the word "No" was eliminated from their vocabulary and instituted a new motto: "Yes is the answer. What is the question?" Afterward he hung pineapple posters in each department to remind the associates of their new motto and encouraged them to find creative and resourceful ways to say *Yes*.

You can only imagine my excitement after reading this article. I loved this story, and as a gal who was young and motivated to change the world, this philosophy truly spoke to my heart. So, with all my excitement, I took this new perspective and went back to my hotel to schedule my very first *Yes Is the Answer* team rally. I told the staff all about the pineapple milkshake article, we served pineapple milkshakes, and we all agreed that our new motto would be, "*Yes* is the answer. What is the question?" Yep, I also hung up pineapple posters in all our departments! The whole team was on board with this new direction, and they were pumped up and passionate about getting to work providing positive responses to our guests.

So, what do you think happened? This is the part where I'm supposed to tell you that it was a perfect success, that our team never said no again, and that our guest service scores reached all-time highs. Well, not exactly. As it turns out, never saying no is super hard! Not only for our associates but also for seasoned managers. My intentions were good; however, merely telling associates that *Yes Is the Answer* and hanging pineapples all over the place wasn't going to make it happen. They needed to know HOW to say *Yes,* and admittedly, I wasn't exactly sure how to always do it myself—*YET!*

Now, after many years of practicing, perfecting, and teaching the art of saying *Yes,* I have concluded that you, too, can learn it in just 32 easy steps. Ha! Just kidding!! It's only *four* simple steps, which I will be outlining in the following chapters.

Are you ready to hear about the four steps to saying *Yes?* Just in case you're still not completely sold, let me offer just a few statistics. Whether you are an entrepreneur, manager, associate, or just trying to keep it positive at home, here are a few other reasons why learning how to respond positively will benefit all aspects of your professional life, and your personal life as well.

- 95 percent of customers share bad experiences with others.[1]
- 58 percent will never use a company again after a negative experience.[2]
- 55 percent of consumers are willing to pay more for a guaranteed good experience.[3]
- 67 percent of customers have left a company due to poor service.[4]
- A 30-year study of 447 people at the Mayo Clinic found that optimists had

around a 50 percent lower risk of early death than pessimists.[5]

Or, as I like to say, "Your margarita can only be as good as your worst lime!" Are you ready to change the world with your *Yes* POWER?!

---

1. https://www.zendesk.com/company/press/zendesk-study-shows-poor-service-frightens-away-customers-years-come-germany/
2. https://www.newvoicemedia.com/en-us/news/corporate/the-multibillion-dollar-cost-of-poor-customer-service
3. https://estebankolsky.com/2015/09/24/want-real-success-destroy-the-company-centric-customer-experience/
4. https://www.toistersolutions.com/blog/2018/5/25/report-poor-customer-service-costs-us-businesses-75-billion
5. https://www.mayoclinicproceedings.org/article/S0025-6196(11)64184-0/abstract https://doi.org/10.4065/75.2.140

SECTION TWO: THE FOUR STEPS

> **Being positive in a negative situation is not naive—it's leadership.**
>
> RALPH MARSTON

3

STEP 1: MAKE FRIENDS FIRST

Optimism is quite possibly one of the most desirable and sought-after attributes. There are probably more self-help books about this than flavors of ice cream. Just to name a few of my favorites: *Delivering Happiness* by Tony Hsieh; *The Front Row Factor* by Jon Vroman; and *Hospitality from the Heart* by Brandon W. Johnson, the Positive Energy Guy. It makes sense, right? Pessimists tend to be cynical, discouraging, and unmotivated. Optimists, on the other hand, tend to be positive, motivated, and always up for a challenge! Which personality would you rather encounter in life—especially in the service industry?

When you approach life from an optimistic

perspective, cultivating good, healthy relationships is generally less challenging. Everything seems easier when you *Lead from the Heart* and can do it with a smile. So, smile and **Make Friends First**, Step 1 in the ***Yes Is the Answer*** philosophy.

We can easily get flustered when someone makes a request for which the seemingly obvious answer is no. We can become so anxious about the prospect of a confrontation that we let it get the better of us. Even before the anticipated question is asked, we often just react and burst out with a no answer. We sense what's coming and want to get it over with as quickly as possible—like ripping off a bandage. Has this ever happened to you? I have both witnessed and experienced this situation many times before.

Here is a perfect example. One busy Tuesday, Janie, one of our top *Cracker Jack* guest service representatives, began her morning shift at 7 a.m. after the hotel had sold out the night before. (I think you might know where I am going with this—there were no clean rooms left in the hotel.) Just then, a smiling guest walked through the front doors with her roller bag. What do you think she was about to ask? Of course—could she have an early check-in?

Before the guest could even reach the check-in desk, Janie said sternly, "Check-in time is at 3 p.m."

Oh, my goodness, I almost fell over! In my head I was yelling, "Wait, Janie. **Make Friends First!**" As you can imagine, that guest's smile quickly disappeared after such an abrupt greeting. Janie, like many service providers, let the anxiety of a potential confrontation catch her off guard, and she reacted negatively as a result.

Would you now like to see how this situation could have turned out much differently by implementing Step 1 of the *Yes Is the Answer* philosophy? GREAT! Before reading on, take a moment to think about Janie's situation. How might you respond positively when asked for an early check-in at 7 a.m. with no rooms available?

_____

_____

_____

Often when I first get started in my workshops,

participants usually begin to answer with "I'm sorry" or "Unfortunately." But those are negative, no-based words.

Here's how the scenario above might look when implementing the *Yes Is the Answer* approach.

Remember Step 1: **Make Friends First**

Guest: Walks in at 7 a.m. and approaches the check-in desk.

Associate: (Suspecting the guest wants an early check-in and knowing there are no rooms available, she takes a breath and greets her guest, **Making Friends First**.) "Welcome. I'm Janie, what brings you to Chicago?"

Guest: "I'm here to check in for my daughter's Navy Graduation."

Associate: "Congratulations! We're so honored to serve our Navy families. May I get your last name to check your reservation?"

Guest: "Thank you, Janie. I'm Mrs. Smith."

Associate: "Wonderful. Mrs. Smith, I see you have a reservation for two nights in one of our spacious king rooms. This room offers a balcony, which overlooks our courtyard with a beautiful view. Your family will love it!" (**Make Friends First!**) "Check-in time is at 3 p.m.; however, I know I will be able to get you into your room early. Here's what I can do. I'll notify housekeeping to put a rush on this room, and I'll get your mobile number to contact you as soon as it's ready. In the meantime, I invite you to enjoy our hotel amenities, or I can hold your bags while you take in some of the local sights! Which works best for you?"

What did you think about that scenario, compared to the first?

Let's take a moment to fully unpack this example. Instead of panicking, knowing that the rooms weren't ready yet, Janie took a breath. She then welcomed her guest, introduced herself, and found out Ms. Smith's name and why she was visiting. In doing these things, she developed a relationship —**Making Friends First** and *Leading from the Heart*. Janie was empowered to stand tall and feel confident, knowing she had created a foundation to build her relationship with this guest. At the same time, Ms. Smith felt appreciated and welcomed. She believed that Janie was on *her* side, rather than the side of the 3 p.m. check-in *rules*. Ms. Smith could clearly see that Janie was doing everything in her power to accommodate her, ensure a great visit, and make her feel special.

This first step may seem ridiculously simple, yet the primary reason for dissatisfied customers is the apprehension that causes service providers to instantly react negatively, and once you start off on the wrong foot, it can be challenging to get back on track.

Additionally, we often say "I'm sorry" when we've done nothing wrong. After all, the check-in time *is* at 3 p.m., right? Randomly apologizing makes the guest think we're not on our game and that the hotel or business is somehow at fault. With Janie's friendly *Yes* approach, she was able to go the extra mile for her guest's special request without apologizing for following the rules. Now Janie also has some great information to connect with this family during their visit. By providing *Sweet Hospitality* and leading from the heart, she can address this guest by name throughout her stay, inquire how graduation went, or even send them a congratulatory note with a special amenity.

PINEAPPLE PRO TIP

Due to technology, there are fewer and fewer opportunities to **Make Friends First** and build a relationship with our guests. Options like online reservations, mobile check-in, and mobile key mean guests can go an entire visit without ever having to stop by the front desk—ever! That's another reason it's imperative that we make every touchpoint unforgettable.

Get it? Got it? Good! Let's get to Step 2!

> I'm not here to be
> good-nuff.
> I'm here to be
> LEGENDARY.

CHRISTINE TRIPPI
"THE WISE PINEAPPLE"

4

STEP 2: TELL THEM WHAT YOU CAN DO!

Words matter! When I visit hotels, I first like to evaluate the need for the *Yes Is the Answer* culture. Typically, I will ask a question that often generates a no answer and see how team members respond. More often than not, the answer comes back "I'm sorry," "No, but …," "I can't," or "Unfortunately." This seems to be something we humans do instinctively. As a result, it takes thoughtful practice to rewire our instincts to say *Yes* and respond positively. Practice makes *permanent* (if not perfect)!

Using positive words such as "*Yes*" makes a difference in our interactions. Speaking in front of a crowd, for example, is one of the top fears among people. *How* we talk about speaking in front of a crowd can dramatically change our results. When we talk about how much anxiety we have or how nervous or afraid we are, we're putting ourselves in a threat mindset. However, when we change our words to the positive, such as how *excited* we are or how *awesome* it will be, we move our brains to an opportunity mindset by thinking about all the things that can go right! A recent study in the *Journal of Experimental Psychology* showed that people who were going to sing karaoke, give a speech, or take a math test all improved when they changed their language from "I am anxious" to "I am excited."[1] Now *that* is exciting!

This attitude change doesn't just apply to new experiences. I recently had a revelation while having coffee with the chief lodging services officer at Marriott International, Erika Alexander. During our conversation, I mentioned that one of my previous bosses took a real risk in hiring me. As we were saying our goodbyes, she said, "I have one piece of advice for you: Avoid saying you were a risk. Maybe at the time you didn't have that experience, but you are an amazing leader, and choosing you isn't a risk. It might have been a *bold* choice or a *daring* move, but *you* weren't a *risk*." I thought, "*Hot damn, Tamale Man!*" Just when you think you're the *Bomb.com* at positive wordsmithing— BOOM! There it is, a new way to add positivity into life. Reframing situations by using positive words changes how you and others view the situation and yourself.

One way to focus on positive words rather than negative words is to tell customers **What You *Can* Do**. You might not be able to do what they are asking, but if you answer with **What You *Can* Do**, you stand tall, are confident, and focus on the positive. Thus, you and the person you're talking to have a better attitude about the experience.

Let's put Step 2, **Tell Them What You *Can* Do**, to the test. Here's another situation I encountered recently.

Upon checking into a suburban hotel, I asked the guest service representative if they offered a shuttle to the airport. The associate responded, "Um, no ma'am. Unfortunately, we do not have a shuttle—not there, not back." True story.

On the surface, it may seem like the associate did the best he could. He was polite, he answered the question truthfully, what else could he do? I mean, how do you say *Yes* to this question? They actually do not have a shuttle!

Let's answer that question—what else *could* he have said? Before doing so, take a minute to reflect on the situation. Can you come up with a way to turn this no into a *Yes*? Here's a hint—start with **Make Friends First!**

_____

_____

_____

_____

Here is how this scenario may have played out using the *Yes Is the Answer* philosophy.

Guest: "Does your hotel have a shuttle to the airport?"

Associate: "Thank you for asking." (**Make Friends First**) "We have a recommended car service that will get you to the airport for only $45." (**What You *Can* Do**). "May I secure a reservation for you?"

So how did you do? Did you find a *Yes* answer on a potentially negative situation? In other words, did you let your pineapple shine?

Keep in mind that for a simple direct question, the first step, **Make Friends First**, might simply be a positive word or opening such as "absolutely" or "thank you for asking!" I understand that some questions and interactions are much quicker and won't call for a full introduction with personalized details; however, if you can add in these elements, all the better! Remember, the phrases "no, but," "I'm sorry," or "unfortunately" are off-limits in the *Yes* game. If you said, "No, but we do have a taxi service," even though you did tell them what you do have, the first thing you actually said was "no!" Let's get rid of the "no, buts!"

Here's another chance to shine up a pineapple:

Let's say you are working at a hotel that doesn't have microwave ovens in their rooms. A guest holding her baby comes to the desk and asks, "Do you have a room with a microwave?" How can you say *Yes* to this guest? You've got this!

SWEET SPOT

How'd you do? Just in case you got stuck, here is how this might look using the *Yes Is the Answer* philosophy.

Guest: "Can I get a room with a microwave?"

Associate: "Thank you for asking! What a darling baby. What's her name? I'll bet she's hungry for a nice warm bottle." (**Make Friends First**) "We do have a microwave available in our market, 24 hours a day. Or if you prefer, I can have a microwave brought to your guest room." (**What You *Can* Do**) "Which works best for you?" And because this associate is a genuine *Yes* leader who leads from the heart, when she delivered the microwave to the guest room, she brought up a little rubber ducky and some baby shampoo as well, building upon that initial relationship. Most of the time associates respond, "No, but I can deliver one to your room." Get rid of those "No, buts!"

Okay, one more quick example. A guest asks for a Diet Coke when you only have Pepsi products. How can you respond *Yes*?

_____

_____

_____

Here are some suggestions:

Guest: "Can I get a Diet Coke?"

Associate: "Oh my gosh, diet pop (*Yes*, I'm from the Midwest) is my go-to caffeine kick, too." (**Make Friends First**) "I'd love to quench your thirst with one of our Pepsi products." (**What You Can Do**) "Does Diet Pepsi work for you?"

See, Pepsi may be all you carry, but you don't have to say, "No, but I can get you a Diet Pepsi," or "I'm sorry, we only carry Diet Pepsi." You don't have to be sorry. Pepsi is a great soft drink! Instead, think of a way to relate to the guest. (**Make Friends First**) Then confidently suggest what you do have. (**What You *Can* Do**)

Get *it? Got it? Good!*

What? Oh, you want to know what happens if the guest says no thanks, they're not a fan of Diet Pepsi? Good question! Let's try it.

Associate: "I'd love to quench your thirst with one of our Pepsi products. May I offer you a Diet Pepsi?"

Guest: "That's okay, actually. I don't like Pepsi products."

Associate: "I completely understand. Thank you for letting me know your preference. I really want you to enjoy your stay with us, so I'll make a point to have some Diet Coke available for you for the remainder of your visit. In the meantime, can I offer you one of these selections?" (Or, *Be Empowered* and have someone run out and get it right then— work that crown! Now that's *Sweet Hospitality!)*

There's always *something* you can do, *true or true?*

As a team, it's crucial to consider what your everyday hard nos are and have plans in place to address them. Be proactive—so many of these situations are foreseeable!

As in my Diet Coke example, if you have customers that regularly ask for Coke products, it makes perfect sense to keep a small stock available for them during their visit. Talk about making friends and building on a relationship! Think about how special that customer will feel when you share your "private stock" of Diet Coke with them.

PINEAPPLE PRO TIP

In each interaction, we saw an opportunity to *Be a Wise Pineapple* and go the extra mile for our customer. We made a taxi reservation, delivered a requested microwave along with some unexpected surprises, and served a customer their preferred beverage. If you are an empowered *Yes* leader who leads from the heart, you'll look for ways to enhance every guest experience to provide *Sweet Hospitality*, and you'll feel amazing doing so!

In most service industries today, satisfaction is now measured by Intent to Recommend (ITR) rather than Overall Satisfaction (OSAT). It's not enough to simply have a good experience anymore. In today's world of social media and online review sites like Trip Advisor, industries need their guests to become advocates! They need them to go out in the world and recommend their product or service to their friends, families, and colleagues.

"Good-nuff" isn't good E-N-O-U-G-H, if you want to be legendary!

---

1. Brooks, Alison Wood. "Get excited: Reappraising pre-performance anxiety as excitement." *Journal of Experimental Psychology: General* 143, no. 3 (2014): 1144.

> If 'Plan 'A' didn't work, the alphabet still has 25 more letters. Stay sweet!

ANONYMOUS

5

STEP 3: OFFER OPTIONS

We've already established that no one likes to be told no. I'm guessing you also would rather not be told what to do. Most people don't care about the rules or laws, but they do care about having their needs and wants met. Basically, we're all pretty much a bunch of three-year-olds running around the globe. We want what we want, when we want it— and we want to be in control!

With that in mind, let's talk about how to help our guests maintain control over every situation by using Step 3 of the *Yes Is the Answer* philosophy —**Offer Options.** You've actually seen this in play in some of our previous examples, but let's focus on it as a specific strategy now. Here is one scenario:

Let's say you're working at the front desk. You

know you have a full hotel for the evening, and the housekeeping team needs to get into the checkout rooms as soon as possible to get them ready for today's arrivals. Suddenly, a guest that's checking out today with a large soccer team just came to the front desk and asked if she could get a late check-out. You recognize that giving one person from this group a late checkout will invite many additional requests, and you can't accommodate them all without putting your operation in jeopardy.

Before reading on, take a minute to think about it. How would you respond with a positive *Yes* answer? Are there any options you can offer?

_____

_____

_____

How'd you do? On the surface that seems like a tough one! Did you remember to implement Steps 1 and 2—**Make Friends First** and consider **What You *Can* Do**? Here's an example of how I might have said *Yes*.

Guest: "Can I get a late checkout?"

Associate: "Absolutely! Thank you for letting me know how I can enhance your visit." (**Make Friends First**) "I'm happy to extend a complimentary 1 p.m. checkout, or if you would like to stay in your room until 3 p.m., it is only $59 plus tax." (**What You *Can* Do**) "Which works best for you?" (**Offer Options**)

I offered a complimentary option and then stated what the charges were for an even later checkout, outlining company policy in a positive (and potentially revenue-enhancing) way. I presented two possible options and then I put the guest back in control by asking which option works best for them. But what really makes this strategy work is what I call my **Magical Question**. When you don't have more than one option available, or if you just can't think of another one in the moment, by asking the question "Does that work for you?" you avoid dictating what your customer must do. Instead, you put the control back into the hands of the customer and allow *them* to decide how *they* want to handle the situation and whether your solution is acceptable to them. See the magic?

Awesome! Right? Say it with me: "*Oooooohhhhhh, Aaaahhhhhhhh, Fabulous!*"

Okay, I know what you're thinking. "That example worked out great, but what if I'm working the front desk and my manager has made it clear that I absolutely cannot extend any additional late checkouts today?"

Great question! I've gotcha covered! We just follow the steps. Let's do this!

Guest: "Can I get a late checkout?"

Associate: "Thank you for giving me the opportunity to enhance your stay, Mrs. Jones. Congratulations to the team for their big win." (**Make Friends First**) "Our hotel is very popular today! What I can do for you is open a meeting room to store all the luggage for anyone staying with your soccer team." (**What You *Can* Do**) "Additionally, I'm happy to extend the team's access to our hotel amenities until 3 p.m." (**Offer Options**) "Will this help your team?"

Any great leader will empower their associates to make these decisions to make it right for the guest and find creative solutions. *Be Empowered—*

wear your crown! There's always *something* you can do!

Okay, you may have thought those last two examples were challenging, but are you ready for a really difficult one? That was a trick question—the answer is *Yes*!

Here is your scenario:

A guest comes to check-in and asks if he can get a smoking room. You are a non-smoking hotel brand, and you do not have any smoking rooms in your hotel. How do you handle it? Write your thoughts below using the three *Yes Is the Answer* steps you've learned so far—**Make Friends First**, consider **What You *Can* Do**, and **Offer Options**. Remember to eliminate the phrases "No, but ...," "I'm sorry," or "Unfortunately ..."

_____

_____

_____

I'm so glad you didn't say, "No. Unfortunately, state law prohibits smoking indoors." Let's review how you might wear your crown and *Be Empowered* to provide a positive *Yes*.

Guest: "Can I get a smoking room?"

Associate: "Thank you for letting me know your request, Mr. Smith. I want you to have an excellent stay!" (**Make Friends First**) "I can place you on the first floor, which will give you quick and easy access to the smoking area." (**What You *Can Do***) "Does this work for you?" (**Offer Options** or **Magical Question.**)

You can see how this interaction promotes confidence, empowerment, and heart and why it would be so much better received by your guest.

I hear you asking what happens if the guest says, "No, actually, that doesn't work for me. I'm on vacation, and I'm not going to be happy unless I can smoke in my room." I know this appears to be very challenging; however, it's not hard at all when you follow the *Yes Is the Answer* steps—simply go back to **Make Friends First**.

Associate: "Mr. Smith, I completely understand, and I want to help make this your best vacation yet!" (**Make Friends First**) "I would be happy to make that a smoking room for you. We will simply place the $250 smoking fee on your bill each day." (**What You *Can* Do**) "Does that work for you?" (**Offer Options** or **Magical Question.**)

Hey, I never said everything we *can* do would be complimentary! Our goal is to stand tall, *Be Confident*, and provide a positive *Yes* answer to deliver upon our customer's needs. And when you're leading from the heart, you genuinely want to help your customer. You may be surprised to learn that I've actually had guests take me up on this offer! Most often, though, they figure the room by the smoking entrance has suddenly become much more agreeable.

Obviously, I'm not advocating the selling of smoking rooms in a non-smoking brand. I use this example, however, to demonstrate that no matter how much a question might scream for a no answer, there really is a *Yes* answer to be found. This is why it's essential to proactively plan for your team's difficult questions and practice, practice, practice!

Let's take our smoking example a step further. Maybe for some reason, even the $250/day smoking fee is simply not an option in your hotel—then what? Is there still another *Yes* answer available to you? How about this example:

Associate: "I completely understand your request and want you to have an amazing vacation, Mr. Smith. I know our hotel will take the best care of you and your family, making you feel at home with our *Sweet Hospitality.*" (**Make Friends First**) "I'm happy to place you in a room on the first floor located by our smoking area, or I would be happy to look for a hotel in the area that offers a smoking room." (**What You *Can* Do**) "Which would work better for your family?" (**Offer Options** or **Magical Question**)

There is no need to say, "No, but … " or "Unfortunately, our state laws prohibit smoking in our guest rooms." Guests don't care about the rules. They care about what their wants and needs are. Stand tall, *Be Confident*, and enthusiastically state **What You *Can* Do**! Even if the customer comes back and says, "So, you don't have any smoking rooms?" you still don't have to say no. Simply re-state what you do have. "That's correct, Mr. Smith. All of our rooms are smoke-free, with several smoking areas available."

Are you thinking that turning away business seems a bit extreme? Listen, if we are looking to *Be a Wise Pineapple* and sincerely *Lead from the Heart*, we want the best for the person we're serving. If you don't have what they need, and they aren't persuaded by the increased benefits of what you do have to offer, then the best thing to do is what's right for your customer. They will appreciate your genuine efforts to satisfy their needs and become even more loyal to your brand or company. However, with heart, always express why your product or service will be the best option.

PINEAPPLE PRO TIP

Take every opportunity you can to use and learn your customer's name. If you're a female reader, I'd like to ask you how you feel when someone says, "Ma'am, ma'am, ma'am!" For me, I like to say, "Only call me ma'am if you're wearing a cowboy hat!"

Dale Carnegie said it best: "A person's name is, to that person, the sweetest, most important sound in any language." When we hear our name, it makes us feel special and valued. It creates a connection with the person who is addressing you and is interpreted as demonstrating more care and empathy. Not to mention it builds loyalty, and people return to where they're known and liked. Take our buddy from *Cheers* for example. The world cheered each episode when the entire bar yelled, "Norm!"

The first and easiest way to learn someone's

name is to introduce yourself and ask for theirs! I have always been taught to use a customer's name three times in an interaction to increase the likelihood I will remember it on the next interaction. The caveat to the importance of using your customer's name is not to overuse it, because it may come off sounding condescending or insincere. So, depending on the situation, you may even want to repeat it silently in your head.

Another trick that worked for me was my own version of the name game. In my head, I would give my guests a positive nickname that started with the first letter of their first or last name. For example, one of my favorite guests was Kool Mr. Kirkland. Depending on the guest, I would use their fun name with them. This works especially well with children, and when you make a child feel special, you hit a home run with mom and dad! If you don't know a guest's name and need to address with a generic title, Sir and Ms. or Miss usually work best, as ma'am can often sound condescending or rude. Can you hear it now? "Ma'am, ma'am, ma'am, I said check-in is at 3 p.m." *Ack!*

Visit my website www.thewisepineapple.com for more Pineapple Pro Tips for learning and using guest names.

> The best way to
> predict the future is
> to create it.

PETER DRUCKER

6

STEP 4: BE CREATIVE

In order to incorporate the first three *Yes Is the Answer* steps into your interactions with customers, you need to **Be Creative**. Sometimes this means brainstorming and being prepared ahead of time. Other times, you'll have to learn to **Be Creative** on the spot. Let's tackle Step 4 of the *Yes Is the Answer* philosophy—**Be Creative.**

The best *Yes* leaders spend time brainstorming with their teams about foreseeable conflicts or dilemmas, and developing strategies for dealing with them before they occur. Remember, practice makes permanent! Just because you know the four steps in your mind, doesn't mean you know them in your mouth. The only way to ensure you will respond positively is if you practice the strategies you've established with each other. Create the potential scenarios that are relevant to your hotel, business, or organization and role-play them; don't just talk about them. The more you do this, the more comfortable and confident you will be when the real-life situation eventually presents itself.

Back in 2011, I was the Director of Fun at the brand new and highly anticipated KeyLime Cove Indoor Waterpark Resort (I know, lucky me!). During our opening weeks, even though I had trained all 654 opening team members in the *Yes Is the Answer* philosophy and proactively addressed every situation we could think of, it wasn't long before we started getting various requests from our guests that we *hadn't* thought of. It's probably fair to say that not everybody who checked in that week felt they had received legendary service during their stay.

But you know what? We didn't see this as a failure but rather as an opportunity. We documented each one of the no obstacles we encountered and brought them to our daily huddle in order to brainstorm *Yes* solutions. One of the biggest issues that came up over and over again had to do with the bell carts. Let me explain.

The resort was vast with 414 guest rooms, multiple retail shops, restaurants, spas, a water park, and more. It was far too large of an establishment to let the guests take the bell carts at will, which so many of them wanted to do. For one thing, the bell carts were the livelihood of our tour guides (bell-men), who needed them to assist guests and earn gratuities. Additionally, how would we ever keep track of who had a cart, given how large the property was? This was a real stumper.

Many times, associates feel they must choose between policy and customer service. Even I, the **Yes Is the Answer** lady, was struggling with how to resolve this! But we collaborated as a team and eventually discovered our *Sweet Spot Yes* answer. Care to try for another shining pineapple with ideas of your own before reading on? How would you respond positively if a guest asked for the bell cart when it was against company policy?

_____

_____

_____

What did you come up with? Here's what we decided to do.

Guest: "Can I grab one of these bell carts?"

Associate: "We're happy to help." (**Make Friends First**) "Every bell cart comes with a complimentary Tour Guide!" (**What You *Can* Do**) "May I send him to your room?" (**Offer Options** or **Magical Question**)

Every single time we delivered that answer, our guests would chuckle and tell us which room we could send the cart to. Using that one simple line—delivered with confidence, humor, enthusiasm, and hospitality—we were able to communicate two messages: 1) That a gratuity was not required, and it was completely their choice and 2) The bell cart alone was not an option. Brilliant, right?!

Here's another example of how to say *Yes* creatively. At the Courtyard by Marriott where I served as general manager, 75 percent of our guests were Marriott Rewards Gold and Platinum status members, and they requested upgrades regularly. Our hotel only had 12 suites, and this proved to be a difficult *Yes* answer for our team. Our ability to work Steps 2 and 3 of **Yes Is the Answer** hinged directly on Step 4—figuring out some creative options to offer once our VIP suites were all gone. (Side note: Marriott's loyalty program is now called Marriott Bonvoy—and it's awesome!)

You know that saying, "If you always do what you always did, you'll always get what you always got"? We had to think differently and look beyond the obvious if we wanted to respond positively. We put our heads together, and eventually I proposed a thought. "Who said that only a suite can be considered an upgrade?" As we talked about it, we realized that anything can be presented as an upgrade as long as the guest feels like they're getting something special—more than they paid or bargained for. Perhaps a guest would prefer a room with a beautiful view of the city or a room with a king bed instead of two doubles, etc. So, our empowered team put their crowns on and brainstormed what our hotel had to offer that could be considered an upgrade.

We were on the right track, but we didn't stop there. We felt we needed a little more, as we were a very busy hotel and typically sold out Monday through Thursday. We continued throwing around ideas, which eventually resulted in the creation of a branded upgrade amenity kit that included enhanced bath amenities, mouthwash, ear plugs, chamomile tea, a bottle of water, a KIND bar, and a stamped postcard from Chicago to send home to the family. Now, when faced with a typical upgrade request that we didn't have available, we always had a *Yes* answer in place to accommodate our guests.

What do you think? *Is that cool or is that cool?*

Let me demonstrate how that might sound in context.

Guest: "Hi, I'm a new Platinum member. Can I get a complimentary upgrade?"

Associate: "Congratulations on your new Elite Platinum status, Ms. Adams!" (**Make Friends First**) "Your new status is very exciting and will award you 25 percent bonus points, 400 additional points upon each check-in, and your choice of a market item or freshly brewed Starbucks coffee! Tonight, I have a fantastic upgraded amenity kit available for you to enjoy. I've also put you in a premium king room that overlooks our beautiful Courtyard." (**What You *Can* Do**) "Doesn't that sound wonderful?" (**Offer Options** or **Magical Question.**)

This is another way to put a situation back in the guest's control—they can tell you whether it's wonderful or not. "Ms. Adams, thank you again for your loyalty to Marriott. We appreciate your business!"

Doesn't that sound significantly better than, "Unfortunately we're sold out tonight and don't have any suite upgrades available"? Remember, *Lead from the Heart.* Now that you know this guest has just achieved her new status, find a way to celebrate and make her feel special. I'll never forget—it was a flight to Phoenix when I achieved United Airlines Platinum Status! Whoa! This was my first big loyalty status for any company and the entire flight I waited for someone to acknowledge this awesome achievement! It never happened! Say it with me … *womp, womp, womp*! When we have information right in front of us that will allow us to make our customers feel special, and we don't use it, it's such a missed opportunity. As Carl W. Buehner eloquently put it, "[People] may forget what you said, but they will never forget how you made them feel."

PINEAPPLE PRO TIP

You don't have to wait for the next department meeting to get innovative—start today! Most hospitality and corporate teams have a huddle or stand-up meeting daily, where the team meets in the beginning of the shift to review the strategies of the day, share information, train, get creative, set goals, and most importantly, recognize each other for great work! This meeting sets the tone for the whole day and should be positive, energetic, and quick—no more than 15 minutes. I would even go so far as to say that your team's huddle is the most important thing you do each day. Legendary teams make the huddle a top priority!

Tune in to my website, The Wise Pineapple, at www.thewisepineapple.com to find *free-sources* such as Pineapple Pro Tips, huddle ideas, and awesome merch!

SECTION THREE: YES LEADERSHIP

"

Great leaders don't set
out to be leaders...
they set out to make a
difference. It's never
about the role—always
about the goal.

UNKNOWN

"

7

BUILDING CONFIDENT LEADERS

Well, my friend, we've just been through the four simple steps, and the pillars of the *Yes Is the Answer* philosophy are: **Make Friends First**, **Consider What You *Can* Do**, **Offer Options** or my **Magical Question**, and **Be Creative**. We've demonstrated and practiced with real-life examples of how you and your team can respond positively *every time!*

This philosophy can be lived each day by anyone who really wants to incorporate optimism in their life—personal or professional. But as an industry professional with a focus on providing *Sweet Hospitality, Sweet Cultures, and Sweet Results,* it is especially important to me to share this with those in any level of hospitality leadership.

We play a vital and important role in shaping the leaders that will follow us. By empowering and teaching your associates how to *Lead from the Heart* and respond positively in every interaction, you give them a powerful gift. You give yourself a gift as well. When they are properly trained and empowered to resolve situations using the **Yes Is the Answer** philosophy, they gain confidence in themselves, which makes them feel valued and trustworthy in return. They become motivated to do their absolute best to create loyal and happy customers, which results in higher guest and associate satisfaction, associate career trajectory, and much happier management (not to mention you're not getting the calls at midnight).

It takes practice to learn a new skill and form good habits, and you'll need to be intentional about where you put your daily focus. Learning to put **Yes Is the Answer** into every interaction may take practice, but little by little, it becomes part of who you are—in this case, a self-assured leader who starts with *Yes*!

Is that cool or is that cool?

These positive behavior strategies don't just apply to your professional life. When you live the **Yes Is** *the Answer* philosophy at work, you'll soon discover it impacting your whole life. How? Because when we *Lead from the Heart* and make someone happy, it makes us happy, too! Think about it. Have you ever found yourself in a situation, personal or professional, where something you were able to do just completely transformed a person's mood from *blah* to joyous? How did it make you feel? Awesome, right?!

Every positive interaction we create has the capacity to create another one. When something good happens to you, aren't you more inclined to do something good for someone else? You've heard the stories about how someone in the fast food line pays the bill for the person behind them, and then 20, 30, 50 cars later the person in front is still paying for the person behind. The ripple effect is real, and you never know how far your ripple will reach … one *Yes* at a time!

Let's visualize confidence and leadership in this actual situation.

Victoria was a somewhat newer associate. A guest approached the front desk and told Victoria her family needed a room for a few weeks because their house caught on fire. They lost everything but, thankfully, everyone was safe. She told Victoria they had a small dog and asked if they could bring little Ralphie to stay with them. Sadly, our hotel brand did not accept pets. Think about being in Victoria's shoes. Although she knew the **Yes Is the Answer** steps, she let the anxiety of the situation throw her off her game. Victoria was about to tell this devastated family, "No, I'm so sorry. Unfortunately, we do not allow pets."

I'd like to ask you to close your eyes for just a moment and think about this transaction. What body language do you think Victoria might have had when delivering this negative response? If you envisioned slouched shoulders, a weak tone of voice, and an unassured or sad facial expression, you would be right. That is exactly how Victoria felt and looked. She was sinking in her confidence with every word. She got stuck and couldn't think of how to respond positively.

When we deliver a negative no answer, it makes us lose our confidence. Instead, we hunch over, stumble over our words, look fragile, and react. The quickest way to cultivate legendary leaders is to teach them *how* to say *Yes*—and practice. The more they practice these strategies, the sooner they can truly *Be a Wise Pineapple* by Standing Tall (*Be Confident*), Wearing their Crown (*Be Empowered*), and Being Sweet (*Lead from the Heart*)! Positive thoughts, emotions, and feelings generate a zing in our step, which spurs us into action and provides solutions!

It's your turn. How would you respond positively to this customer asking to bring her family pet when your hotel does not allow pets?

_____

_____

_____

How did you do? If you followed the four steps, I know you did great! After this actually happened, I worked with Victoria to think about what we *could* do in this scenario.

Step 1: **Make Friends First**. Even when you instantly feel stuck, always take a breath and **Make Friends First**. This act of kindness will lead you to those can-do solutions. Empathize with Mrs. Ward about her family's situation, ensure her you're going to do everything you can to get them settled and take care of their needs. Oh, and pay special attention to their pup, asking his name, petting him, etc.

Step 2: **Tell them What You *Can* Do**. "What I can do is make accommodations for your family to stay with us, and I can make a reservation for little Ralphie at our local pet hotel. They are a fantastic facility that I would absolutely use for my dog, Max. Is this something that would work for your family?" (**Magical Question**)

Step 3: **Offer Options**. If that doesn't sound good for the guest, here is another option (and the one our guest chose, by the way). "Mrs. Ward, I completely understand you want little Ralphie to be with the family. (**Make Friends First**) I've just called the Residence Inn, our sister property. They are a pet-friendly hotel and they have a two-room suite available. This way your whole family can stay together. (**What You *Can* Do**) Does this work better for you?" (**Magical Question**)

This guest was so relieved. She just needed someone to take care of her and her family as she simply had too much else going on to deal with all the accommodations as well. It was such an honor to help this family get settled in their temporary home. After we made Mrs. Ward's arrangements and sent her and her family on their way, we asked the team at the Residence Inn to prepare the room with a special treat and welcome card from all of us at the Courtyard as a sweet surprise. In addition, while their house was being completed, we stayed in touch with the Ward family and even helped arrange a pet parade at the Residence Inn, in which Ralphie took lead. There is always something extra you can do to change the world, one *Yes* at a time. Can I get a *whoop-whoop* for difference makers!?

PINEAPPLE PRO TIP

Are you thinking, "Man, the last thing I need is to say *Yes* more. I'm one of those people that says *Yes* to everything, and my life is a crazy mess because of it." Well, my friend, this philosophy can actually help you, too! I'm sure you've read advice that says you should say no without any explanations; however, if that felt right to you, you wouldn't be in this situation in the first place, *true or true?* Let me offer this example: Say your child's school has asked you to volunteer for yet another fundraiser. Just follow the four steps, "Thank you for your trust in me." (**Make Friends First**) "I am happy to make a donation, as I am scheduled for pie baking on the 6th." (**What You *Can* Do**) "Will this help the cause?" (**Offer Options** or **Magical Question**) You were confident, genuine, friendly, and maintained a relationship, all while setting your boundaries and not letting anyone take advantage of you.

Like it? Love it? Let's Live it!

> **Leadership is not about being in charge. Leadership is about taking care of those in your charge.**
>
> SIMON SINEK

8

TWO CUSTOMERS

In our businesses, we have two types of customers. The customer who pays us and the customer whom we pay. That's right, our associates. It's not okay to be delivering positive, legendary service to our paying customers and then react negatively when an associate asks for something. How can you expect your associates to treat your customers with *Sweet Hospitality* if *their* service isn't so *sweet*?

In today's world, there simply is no question about the impact of having a first-in-class company culture. Researchers in the Department of Economics at the University of Warwick found that happy workers are 12 percent more productive than the average worker, and unhappy workers are 10 percent *less* productive.[1] In fact, unhappy employees cost American businesses more than $300 billion each year. So, if you want *Sweet Results*, it literally pays to put your associates first and make sure they're happy.

J.W. and Alice Marriott founded their company on a philosophy of putting people first. J.W. said, "If you take care of your people, they will take care of your customers, and the business will take care of itself." When I had the honor to meet his son, Mr. Bill Marriott, I asked him if he could give general managers one piece of advice, what would that be. Mr. Marriott looked me right in the eyes and said with absolute conviction, "I'd say to take care of your people!" My friend, he is the *real deal* and meeting him was one of the highlights of my entire career—*cool or cool?!*

Let me set the scene for an associate *Yes Is the Answer* scenario:

Associate: "Hi Boss, I'd really like to have my weekends with family. Can I work Monday through Friday and have weekends off?" (If you're a person in charge of schedules in hospitality, I'll give you a minute to get up off the floor.)

Before you continue, use your new skills to practice how you would respond positively.

_____

_____

_____

How did you do? If we just react and don't take that breath, it might come out like this:

Manager: "Have all weekends off? Are you _nuts_? This is a hotel! Get out of my office!" I know that might be what some leaders might immediately think, but please take a breath and **Make Friends First**.

Here is how this encounter might look using the *Yes Is the Answer* philosophy.

Manager: "Come on in, Samantha. Thank you for coming to see me about this. Congratulations again on your awesome guest comment last week.

You're doing a great job." (**Make Friends First**) "I can understand why you would want weekends off. Let's first look at what weekend is most important to you, and I'll make sure that particular one is cleared for your celebration. However, as a working family, we need to consider the whole team. If you can work with your teammates and all agree that they will cover every weekend so you can work Monday through Friday, then *Yes*, you absolutely can have weekends off." (**What You *Can* Do**) "Why don't you reach out to your coworkers and see what you can work out? In the meantime, I'm going to make sure you're scheduled off for your requested weekend. Does that work for you?" (**Offer Options** or **Magical Question**)

Isn't this a much more courteous way to respond than what you might originally have been thinking? A respected and nurtured associate will respect and nurture their colleagues and guests!

At the end of the day, *Yes Is the Answer* is about leading from the heart and approaching each situation in a positive, solution-focused way, and the four steps help you get there. This doesn't just work in hospitality; it works in any facet of your life:

business, school, organizations, or home. Here's an example for home. Let's say your son asked to use the car on Saturday night. Many of us moms and dads might react immediately in a negative or suspicious way: "Where are you going?" "Who are you going with?" "Why do you need the car?" When you respond like this, your son automatically becomes defensive. What if we took a breath and **Made Friends First**?

Mom: "Thank you for asking first." (This immediately diffuses the situation by making friends and not jumping into why this won't be possible.) "Can I get a little bit more information about the time you'll need the car? I have an appointment until 6 p.m., so you can use it after then; however, I'd like you home by 11 p.m." (**What You *Can* Do**) "Will that work for you?" (**Offer Options** or **Magical Question**—Her son will feel in control, and when you feel in control you are much more cooperative because you're not being told what you *must* do.)

If I'm being honest, following the four steps came very naturally for me at work; however, at home it took more practice. Things can be much more emotional at home, but sharing this technique with the whole family can help build your relationships and begin empowering your kids to become awesome, confident leaders! Can I get a double whoop on getting along with teenagers!? *Whoop-whoop!*

PINEAPPLE PRO TIP

Did you know the number one reason people leave a job is that they don't feel appreciated? In fact, according to one Gallup survey, only three in 10 U.S. employees strongly agreed that they had received recognition or praise for doing good work in the last seven days.[2] A great book to check out is *1001 Ways to Reward Employees* by Bob Nelson. As you read through the book and find great ideas that will work for you, put them right into your electronic calendar throughout the year, so they'll pop-up and remind you to execute! You can even set them up to recur weekly, monthly, or yearly.

As I've mentioned already, your daily huddle is the most important thing you do. Ending each huddle with shout-outs will provide an opportunity for the team to recognize each other every single day! Legendary teams make this part of their *Sweet Culture.* You can visit my website, The Wise Pineapple, at www.thewisepineapple.com to download a free list of my favorite ways to recognize associates and access other *free-sources*!

---

1. Oswald, Andrew J., Eugenio Proto, and Daniel Sgroi. "Happiness and productivity." *Journal of Labor Economics* 33, no. 4 (2015): 789-822. https://doi.org/10.1086/681096
2. https://www.gallup.com/workplace/231659/performance-measures-motivate-madden-employees.aspx?g_source=EMPLOYEE_ENGAGEMENT&g_medium=topic&g_campaign=tiles

SECTION FOUR: THE YES CULTURE

"

The two things you
are in total control
over are your
attitude and your
effort.

BILLY COX

"

9

YES SPEAK!

As I started to touch on in Chapter Four, 90 percent of our service is *how* we say things. Saying *Yes* doesn't always mean literally saying "*Yes.*" Other ways include "absolutely," "certainly," "it's my pleasure," and "what I can do is…" I always had a small sign at the front desk with a few of these words and phrases to help remind associates of other ways to say *Yes*. Transition words are also important because just as you are delivering a great response, you can create that major letdown by inserting "unfortunately."

"I'd love to help you; unfortunately, I can't."

Rather than saying "but" or "unfortunately," use a positive transition word such as "however."

Let's take this scenario, which was one of the

hardest no questions my associates at the Courtyard faced.

Guest: "I'm a Platinum member, so isn't breakfast free?"

For an additional charge, the Courtyard brand has a Bistro that helps you "Make Room for a Little Fun" by offering breakfast, cocktails, Starbucks beverages, and dinner. Other Marriott Select brands provide complimentary breakfast, so it's understandable how this could be confusing to some guests. How would you respond positively if a Platinum guest asks if breakfast is complimentary, when it isn't?

SWEET SPOT · SWEET SPOT · SWEET SPOT · SWEET SPOT

_____

_____

_____

Did you let your pineapple shine? Here's how I coached my team to respond to this challenging question. Remember, don't let the anxiety of the question get you off-track. Take a breath and **Make Friends First**.

Associate: "Mr. Baldridge, thank you for being an Elite Platinum member. We appreciate your loyalty." (**Make Friends First**) "As part of your Elite benefits, you'll receive 400 bonus points upon check-in, upgraded internet, and a freshly brewed Starbucks beverage. However, I can place your breakfast right on your room bill for you." (**What You *Can* Do**) "Does that work for you?" (**Offer Options** or **Magical Question**) Did you see how the transition word "however" is much more palatable than "unfortunately" or "but"? Read it again, replacing "however" with "unfortunately." Big difference! Avoiding negative words like "can't," "won't," or "don't" can increase personal or business interactions.

Another speaking pattern that many of us fall prey to is telling people what we ***don't*** want them to do. Did you know that the brain cannot process the word "don't?" What if I were to say to you, "Don't think about a hot fudge sundae with walnuts and whipped cream, topped with a sweet, red cherry?" You thought about it, didn't you? Your brain hears everything that you and others say after "don't."

I learned this at a workshop by Ann Simmons, and once I became aware, I caught myself doing it. I stopped in my tracks when I heard myself say to my daughter, "*Don't* text and drive." I immediately changed the conversation to the positive behavior I wished to see: "Please, drive safely." It also helps to form this habit when you start with, "I like it when you ..." (**Make Friends First**) This approach is also a lot less defensive and accusatory, and it comes from the heart.

As I started to focus more on the positive behaviors I was looking for, I saw this language pop up in other areas of my communication, such as my emails and text messages. As I typed an email, I saw it: "We should never ..." I caught myself starting with a negative! I immediately backspaced over those words and changed my tone to reflect the positive behavior I wanted to see, rather than the negative behavior I didn't want to see. You are now aware of these key strategies and having awareness comes with responsibility: a responsibility to act!

Get it? Got it? Good!

PINEAPPLE PRO TIP

It's not just what you say, but how you say it! If you have a sarcastic tone of voice or defensive, sloppy body language, it's going to impact the sincerity of your message. Are you familiar with Albert Mehrabian's now-debunked 55-38-7 Rule of Personal Communication? He did a study in 1967, which found that 55 percent of what people hear is your body language, 38 percent is your tone of voice, and only 7 percent is what you actually say. While his study may have been misinterpreted by the masses over the years, it's clear that body language and tone of voice make a significant impact on the message you're trying to convey, and it's important to have self-awareness and help others you lead to be self-aware of all three communication methods.

Yes **Speak:**

Cut That / Say This

Cost / Fee Investment

Transfer / Connect

Here You Go / Here You Are

Problem / Opportunity

Risk(y) / Bold or Daring

You Should / Consider

No Problem / My Pleasure

Criticism / Feedback

Don't / I Like it When

Stubborn / Persistent or Committed

Bossy / Leader

Impatient / Eager

Manipulative / Negotiator

I'll Try / I Will

I'm Sorry / Thank You for Your Patience

I Have To / I Get To

> Where focus goes,
> energy flows.

TONY ROBBINS

10

THE ESSENCE OF YES!

I hope that by now you're feeling excited and inspired! Before you begin your *Yes* adventure, I want to talk about the essence of *Yes*! It is important to not only deliver the **Yes Is the Answer** steps, but to also deliver them from the heart with a genuine spirit of kindness and hospitality to maximize the chance of getting the results you want.

Being a *Yes* leader begins with heart and the right attitude. There are thousands of studies that prove how positive thinking can boost your skills, improve your health, and broaden your opportunities—and it all starts with your thoughts. As Mahatma Gandhi said, "A man is but the product of his thoughts. What he thinks he becomes." Your thoughts become your words, your words become your actions, your actions become your daily routine, and your daily routines become your results. This works both ways, whether your thoughts are positive or negative.

Some people think all this "positive energy" stuff is a bunch of fluff; however, it is 100 percent real and it is backed by science! This is all part of the Reticular Activation System (RAS), which was discovered by Moruzzi, Magoun, and their colleagues in 1949.[1] Let me briefly explain in a way that's easy to understand. You've heard of "the law of attraction" or "self-fulfilling prophecy"? That is the RAS at work. It's a group of nerves in the base of our brain which acts together to filter out 99.9 percent of the information around us that we see, smell, or hear. Our conscious brain can only handle about 130 messages per second and only two in any meaningful way. Your RAS filter only lets through what it thinks is important. It decides what's important by what you *focus* on, and then it sets out to prove you're right.

Think of it like this. The RAS has a "thinker" part and a "prover" part. The "thinker" is the bit that asks the questions or sets an intention (what you focus on), and the "prover" is the one serving up the information to answer the question or prove you're right. Whatever you say or ask yourself becomes your focus. So, for example, if you wake up late and say, "Oh God, this is going to be a horrible day," you've put that in your thinker, and the prover will work to prove you right all day! You know how they say bad things happen in threes? That's the prover. Once something bad happens and you start looking for two more bad things (because you think everything bad happens in threes), your prover *will* find those two additional bad things. However, if you decide to look for something good to counter the bad event that just happened instead, the same will be true—your prover will set out to find something good!

Here's another example: Have you ever bought a new car and suddenly you're seeing that car everywhere? That's the RAS at work. Your new car is now in your focus. Since I began *The Wise Pineapple*, I now see pineapples EVERYWHERE! A great book to read on the RAS is *Switch on Your Brain* by Dr. Caroline Leaf. Whatever you direct your RAS to focus on will become your reality. You can literally create your reality. This is great news! Every day we get to decide how our day goes— positive life or negative life—the choice is yours!

Are you pickin' up what I'm droppin'?

THE EMPOWERMENT CIRCLE

THOUGHTS

WORDS

RESULTS

YOUR
CROWN

ACTIONS

ROUTINE

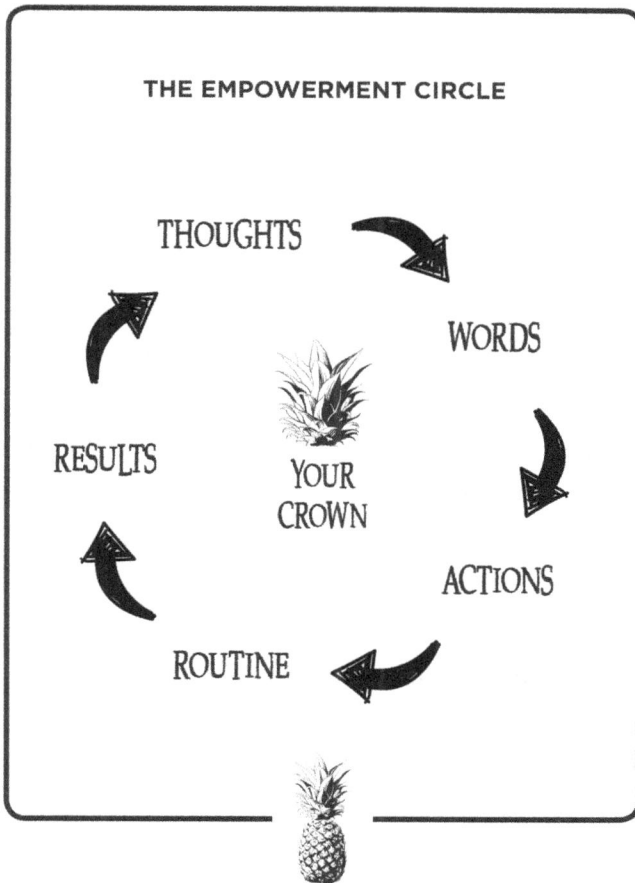

PINEAPPLE PRO TIP

Often our daily habits can get in the way of our energy. What can you add or remove to help create positive energy in your life? For example, do you drive to work listening to the talking heads (not the music group, the political news heads)? No matter what side of the aisle you lean to, it probably generates some negative energy, and when you arrive at your destination that energy is bound to show through. Can you change up your morning routine to listen to a TED Talk? Listen to music that pumps you up? Listen to a leadership book, like this one? What else can you add to your daily routine to fill your energy tank?

Remember, in order to be there for the people in your life, you first have to take care of *you*! How about starting each day writing in a gratefulness journal, meditating, or exercising rather than scrolling through Facebook? One of my favorite routines is to start my day off sending a note of appreciation to someone in my life. Remember, the energy you put out comes back to you, and that is super cool! Hal Elrod said in his fantastic book, *The Miracle Morning*, "Those who only do what they feel like ... don't do much. To be successful at anything you must take action even when you don't feel like it, knowing that the action itself will produce the motivation you need to follow through."

---

1. Moruzzi G, Magoun HW., Brain stem reticulata formation and activation of the EEG. Electroencephalogr Clin. *Neurophysiol.*I :455-473, 1949. Reprinted in:*J Neuropsychiatry Clin Neurosci.* Spring 1995, 7 (2) :251-67, PMID 7626974

> Ideas don't make you legendary, the execution of ideas does.

UNKNOWN

11

FOND FAREWELL

Well, my friend, it's been an honor to share with you the **Yes Is the Answer** philosophy and how to *Be a Wise Pineapple*—Stand Tall (*Be Confident*), Wear a Crown (*Be Empowered*), and Be Sweet (*Lead from the Heart*). So, what now? You've read the book and my hope is that you're energized and ready to begin your *Yes* journey to experience *Sweet Hospitality, Sweet Cultures, and Sweet Results!*

Something I learned from my friend Brandon W. Johnson, The Positive Energy Guy, is that Energy x Execution = Results! Right now, you might be feeling energized; however, we know what is waiting for us when we close this book—the whirlwind!

To break through anything, we need to first identify it, own it, and then act on it. You have identified the need to respond positively, you've owned it by practicing your skills here in this book, and now it's time to act! When you identify and make a commitment, the likelihood that you will complete it significantly increases when you write it down.

Take a moment to write down an "I will" commitment for what you *will* do to teach and apply the **Yes Is the Answer** philosophy in your life. Whether it be with family, friends, team, customers, or colleagues, it's time to say *Yes*! Remember to use the hashtag #yesistheanswer on social and get *freesources* at my website www.thewisepineapple.com to help you along the way.

I WILL:

_____

_____

_____

I began this book by sharing with you that my life's

ambition was to change the world through *Sweet Hospitality*. It's an optimistic purpose and one I hope speaks to you as loudly as it does to me because just imagine how much of a difference we could make if we did it together – one *Yes* at time!

Oooohhhh, Aaaahhhhhh, Fabulous!

TRIP-TACULAR **VERNACULAR Glossary**

- *Wise Pineapple* — A smart hospitality person who is confident and empowered and leads from the heart!!
- *Sweet Hospitality, Sweet Cultures, and Sweet Results!* — What you'll get if you hire Christine Trippi for training, consulting, or speaking at your event!
- *Sweet Spot* — The perfect balance of professional and fun, while doing a little extra!
- *Wear a Crown* — When you empower yourself to be a LEADER!
- *Shine your pineapple* — Every time you find a way to say *Yes*, it makes you sparkle!
- *Hot damn, Tamale Man!* — This is said or thought at a moment of brain-altering enlightenment!
- *Bomb.com* — The absolute BEST. This isn't the same as the bomb.net.
- *Is that cool or is that cool?* — There is no option; that's cool stuff!
- *True or True* — Again, no dispute. That statement is fact! (I borrowed this one from the awesome Brandon W. Johnson! Thanks, Brandon!)

- ***Your margarita is only as good as your worst lime*** — One sour associate attitude can make the whole team look bad.
- ***Oooooohhhhhh, Aaaahhhhhhh, Fabulous!*** — This one is pretty self-explanatory, but to get the full effect you must really drag out the Ooh and Aah!
- ***Are you pickin' up what I'm droppin'?*** — Are you buying in to this concept?
- ***Are you buyin' what I'm sellin'?*** — Do you feel like this information is valuable?
- ***Get it? Got it? Good!*** — I'm so passionate about *Sweet Hospitality* that I talk fast and can get ahead of myself. I use this to make sure my audience is still with me!
- ***Free-sources*** — All the sweet free goodies I have waiting for you at my website, www.thewisepineapple.com
- ***Good-nuff*** — The effort is so mediocre, it's not even worth spelling it out.
- ***Whoop-Whoop*** — M A J O R E N T H U S I A S M!!!
- ***Whoop!*** — Half the enthusiasm as Whoop-Whoop. However, still a lot of E N T H U S I A S M!

- *Cracker Jack* — An associate that is so good at what they do, they're as good as, if not better than, Cracker Jacks.
- *No, buts* — What people used to say before reading *Yes Is the Answer*!

Whoop—whoop! You've finished the book! Thanks for having fun and learning with me!

Be Sweet,
Christine Trippi, "The Wise Pineapple"

ABOUT THE AUTHOR

Christine Trippi is an award-winning hospitality leader who began her hotel career at the age of 17 as a van driver/laundry girl, and her specialty has become moving red hotels to GREEN! She has spent more than 30 years working in hotel operations for companies such as Marriott, Hilton, Crown Plaza, and Courtyard by Marriott, where she was named General Manager of the Year. As the founder of The Wise Pineapple LLC, Christine inspires and helps leaders and organizations to *Be Confident, Be Empowered, and Lead from the Heart*—achieving *Sweet Results!*

Christine was raised and still resides in the Chicagoland area with her husband, Mike (aka Bunny) and her two awesome kids, Spencer and Samantha. When Christine isn't working, she is most likely doing something that terrifies her husband, like jumping out of planes, taking a selfie on top of a mountain, or talking to strangers. Christine likes her nails pink, her Diet Coke with Captain, and her hugs BIG!

To learn more or to book Christine for your next event or workshop, visit TheWisePineapple.com or ChristineTrippi.com.

www.ingramcontent.com/pod-product-compliance
Lightning Source LLC
Chambersburg PA
CBHW050528190326
41458CB00045B/6745/J